HOW

TO

BEACH

H O W T O B E A C H

13-Digit ISBN: 978-1-64643-429-9
10-Digit ISBN: 1-64643-429-3

This book may be ordered by mail from the publisher. Please include $5.99 for postage and handling. Please support your local bookseller first!

Books published by Cider Mill Press Book Publishers are available at special discounts for bulk purchases in the United States by corporations, institutions, and other organizations. For more information, please contact the publisher.

Cider Mill Press Book Publishers
"Where good books are ready for press"
501 Nelson Place
Nashville, Tennessee 37214

cidermillpress.com

Printed in China

Typography: Adobe Text Pro, Poppins

All vectors and images used under official license from Shutterstock.com and Unsplash.com.

23 24 25 26 27 DSC 5 4 3 2 1
First Edition

HOW

TO

BEACH

THE PROFESSIONAL
BEACHGOER'S GUIDEBOOK

TIM RAYBORN

CIDER MILL
PRESS

BOOK
PUBLISHERS

CONTENTS

INTRODUCTION 6

PREPARING FOR PARADISE 10

TIKI COCKTAIL RECIPES 34

HEALTH & SAFETY 58

FUN IN THE SUN 98

ARE YOU SHORE WE HAVE TO LEAVE? 142

ONLINE RESOURCES 156

INTRODUCTION

Everyone loves the beach! Well, maybe not everyone, but there's no doubt that going to the beach—whether as a day trip from home, or as the centerpiece of whole vacations—is something that many people just can't get enough of. Resorts around the world cater to millions of visitors who are eager to escape cold weather (or at least the humdrum of their home-towns) and relax somewhere with white, sandy beaches, clear blue water, hot weather, and the sounds of surf and sea. If you're one of them, then this book is for you.

The first question you'll need to answer is: Is your beach adventure a single day trip or more? Are you planning a whole vacation around visiting a beach or several beaches, or are you just looking for an enjoyable day out? It might seem obvious, but the difference between these two will influence the choices you make about where you're going and what you'll be doing. While this book can be used for either option, it's a little bit more geared toward day trips, though much of its information can be helpful for longer and more ambitious vacations too.

You've no doubt spent a lot of time at beaches in the past, so you might think you don't need a little book like this; however, this guide will help you plan your next beach trip more efficiently, and maybe give you a chance to consider things you'd not thought of before. It offers you tips for choosing the right beach, information on tides and water safety, a list of some of the best surfing beaches around the world, how to plan for emergencies and mishaps, fun activities to do in colder weather, and many other useful bits of information. There's even an entry on nude beaches, if you dare!

As you'll see, there's so much more to the beach than just sitting in the sun, soaking up rays, and going for a dip. Whether you are at the ocean or by a lake, on a foreign trip or a domestic one, or out for a day or for two weeks, this book will help you get the most out of your next beach adventure.

PREPARING FOR PARADISE

FINDING THE RIGHT BEACH

Searching for the right beach might feel a little bit like a treasure hunt (or maybe finding a needle in a haystack). It all depends on what you're looking for. With countless different kinds of beaches out there, it will be up to you to decide what you want from your beach trip. You might also be limited by what beaches are in your area, whether you have access to ocean beaches or to lake beaches, and so on. Keeping all that in mind, here are some ideas for helping you narrow down your search.

ASK YOURSELF WHAT IT IS YOU WANT FROM YOUR DAY OUT. Do you like quiet places, or do large crowds not bother you? Your answer will eliminate a number of possibilities right away. Some people love sitting on a huge beach that has throngs of other beach lovers milling about and doing their own thing (think all those Southern California beaches from *Baywatch* and other TV shows and movies). These party people like to soak up the atmosphere around them as much as the sun's rays. But for others, the idea of being surrounded on all sides with noise and constant activity will be excruciating. Do you want quiet, or busy, or something in between? If you're going with friends or family, what do they want? You might all have to make some compromises.

CHECK INTO EASE OF ACCESS. Some beaches are easy to get to, and some require that you park far away and walk. You might have to go down a slope to get to the beach, and thus back up when you leave. What is best for you? If you have kids or any physical limitations, this might be a serious consideration. What kind of shape are you in? Are you up for dragging a day's worth of items with you on a long trek out to a beach? If not, find something that's easier to get to. If you're visiting by public transportation, this is even more of an issue, especially if you have children with you. And speaking of kids...

PICK SOMEWHERE CHILD FRIENDLY. You'll want to pick someplace that is kid friendly, has safe enough water for children to splash about in, has lifeguards on duty, and so on. A good, soft, sandy beach is going to be much more kid friendly for a classic day out than one that is rocky and gravelly, unless you're specifically going to check out tidal pools, or some other nonswimming adventure.

PICK SOMEWHERE PET FRIENDLY. Your dog might love nothing more than a chance to get out and tear up the sands, but make sure that the beach is a safe place for animals, and that they are permitted to be there. Animals can inadvertently harm local wildlife, and many beaches do not allow pets, mainly dogs.

WHAT IS THE PURPOSE OF YOUR TRIP?
This might have more answers than you think. Are you

there to lap up the sun's rays? Go swimming? Head out for some surfing? Go for a jog? Play volleyball or another game? Do some combination of all of these things? Remember, the more you want to do, the more gear you'll need to bring. Be realistic about what you can do in a day, and plan accordingly. Some beaches might be ideal for certain activities, but not others. If you can't do everything you want at one beach, it's perfectly okay to set aside some activities for another location and time later on. Also on that note...

NOT EVERY ACTIVITY IS PERMITTED AT EVERY BEACH. Check to make sure that the things you want to do are allowed. While most beaches allow swimming, some don't permit surfing, for example, or more vigorous sports like jet skiing. In some places, snorkeling might be fine, while in others, it might be too dangerous, or the local sea life might be too fragile. Beach volleyball might be just the thing at one location, but an annoying nuisance at another.

BE MINDFUL OF SHARKS AND OTHER SEA CREATURES. These animals are not normally a problem in most places, but at some times of the year, there might be migrations of animals (such as whales) passing through, or there might be warnings posted about dangers in the water (such as jellyfish or toxic algae blooms). Shark attacks are very rare—seriously, you're more likely to be injured by a cow, statistically speaking—but jellyfish and other dangers do pop up in the ocean from time to time, more frequently than you might like. Be sure to check into any safety warnings at your target beach before you go, and read up on the safer and more dangerous times of the year to visit, if any.

WHEN WILL YOU BE GOING? Obviously, if you are limited to weekends, the beach is probably going to be a lot more crowded than on a weekday, especially in summer. But if you do have the luxury of going on a weekday, or you're on a vacation that is not at the busiest time of year, you'll probably have more of the place to yourself. Make sure that you plan ahead for weekend or holiday traffic and other potential delays. You don't want to spend half your day sitting in traffic!

W H A T   T O   W E A R

The beach clothing you choose will depend on many different factors. Assuming that you'll be going in the summertime, or at least during warm weather, your choices are already narrowed down quite a bit. You probably already have some good ideas about what to wear, and maybe your own favorite clothes that you're already using, but here are some additional suggestions.

WEAR WHAT YOU FEEL MOST COMFORT-ABLE IN. There is no such thing as a "beach body," and this is not a contest, with others or with yourself. If you feel good about wearing a revealing swimsuit, then by all means, do so. But if not, it's perfectly fine to wear whatever kind of swimwear makes you feel good. If you don't want to wear swimming clothing at all, that's perfectly fine too. Many people like to just go to the beach to take in the atmosphere, listen to the water, and relax.

BRING EXTRA CLOTHES TO CHANGE INTO. This might seem obvious, but it's something that people often forget. Of course, if you're going to be swimming or otherwise out in the water and the sand, you'll want to wear one set of clothes to the beach and then change into your beach outfit. Then you'll want to change back afterward. Most beaches have outdoor showers where you can wash off the sea salt and sand, so at least you're not bringing back all the grit in your clothes!

MAKE SURE YOUR CLOTHING IS UV RESISTANT. Yes, you'll be wearing sunscreen too (and if not, you absolutely need to!), but having an extra layer of sun protection is never a bad idea.

BRING A LIGHT, WIDE-BRIMMED HAT. You might be afraid that you'll look a bit like a rustic, historical farmer, but think about it: they were out in the fields all day, and hats like these kept the sun off their faces and out of their eyes. Be like an old-time farmer—wear the hat.

BRING A FEW MESH BAGS TO PUT YOUR WET CLOTHES IN. You'll want someplace to store your clothing. Mesh bags are lightweight and quick drying. Just be sure to brush off as much sand as you can from your swimwear beforehand, so that you don't bring home a healthy amount in your car!

WEAR SOMETHING ON YOUR FEET. It can be fun to frolic barefoot in the sand, but remember that sand can get very hot in the sun, and you don't want to burn the soles of your feet just because it looked like fun in the moment. Also, sand can conceal sharp rocks and pieces of glass. Cutting your foot on the beach will ruin your day. As for what kinds of footwear...

WEAR LIGHT, WATERPROOF SHOES OR BEACH SANDALS. It's worth investing in some good ones that you can wear for several years. They will give you some decent foot protection. Shop for them just as you would for regular shoes: look for a good fit, decent arch support, a good grip on the soles, and so on. Also, be sure to get water-resistant shoes that are also quick drying, so you won't be sloshing around in wet footwear all afternoon.

WEAR SOME CHEAP RUBBER FLIP-FLOPS WHEN YOU GO WALKING ABOUT. They aren't especially comfortable for anything more than short trips, but at least they provide some protection. Consider getting some better shoes if you're going to be spending more than a day or two each year at a beach.

INVEST IN SOME GOOD SUNGLASSES. It's not enough to protect your skin; you need to protect your eyes as well. Beaches can be very bright, especially if the sand is light colored, and the sun reflecting off the surface can be blinding. Plus, sunlight over time can damage the eyes, just as it damages the skin. So in order to ensure comfort for your eyes and not having to squint all day, get the sunglasses. You probably already have a good pair, but if not, make sure that you get glasses that provide proper UVA and UVB protection, preferably 99% blockage and up. It's worth considering getting polarized lenses, since they block glare and provide 100% protection from UVA and UVB. Polarized lenses are great for driving too. When shopping, check the glasses for information on how much radiation they filter and whether or not they are polarized. If the tag doesn't tell you, move on to one that does. As for styles, large, wraparound lenses offer more protection than smaller and thinner designs.

WHAT TO BRING

In addition to obvious things like swimwear and sunscreen, what other essentials should you bring with you? Again, it will depend on the type of day out you're planning, but here are some basics that no beachgoer should be without.

ALWAYS HAVE ZIPLOC BAGS AND SMALL TRASH BAGS. Ziploc bags allow you to store items and keep water and sand out, while trash bags will be essential even if the beach has its own garbage cans on-site (which is likely). That way, you can easily dispose of all of your waste items. Please don't leave anything behind! Leave the beach exactly as you found it.

BRING QUICK-DRYING MESH BAGS. Again, these are great for carrying clothing that you'll change into and out of at the beach. A waterproof tote bag is another option.

USE DISTINCT TOWELS. That way, you'll be able to recognize them if you decide to take a swim or walk. The more colorful and unusual, the better! Are they large enough to cover the sand so you can sit comfortably? Do you have towels that are big enough to get you fully dry after your dip in the water? Don't skimp and get tiny towels—wrap yourself up in luxury! You'll be glad you did. Just remember that too many towels can get heavy to carry, especially if they have some water in them, so plan accordingly.

CONSIDER BRINGING COMFORTABLE, LIGHTWEIGHT SEATING. You might think you'll be content with just spreading out a big beach towel, but you'll probably find that as the day wears on, you'll get tired. While a big towel is a must, also consider bringing portable seats or reclining chairs, such as "gravity free" recliners or loungers that you can relax in. This is especially true if you have children who might get tired or bored. Consider the type of portable chair you'll want. Does it have its own shade? Some do. Does it have drink holders? That might be nice! Is it light enough to carry for some distance? You'll be glad for it if you have to!

CHECK INTO UMBRELLAS. Does the beach have sun umbrellas, or do you need to bring your own? Some beaches have them, but not all. You should not be sitting in direct sun all day, especially between 10:00 a.m. and 4:00 p.m., so having reasonable shade is a must. There are some amazing sun shelters today, such as beach tents and easy-to-assemble pop-up tents that provide great shade and a nice place to sit.

ALWAYS BRING A FIRST AID KIT IN A WATERPROOF CONTAINER. Even if there is a lifeguard on duty, you'll want to have some things on hand to help with small mishaps, which are almost inevitable the more often you go to any beach! Your first aid kit should include: pain relief (aspirin and/or ibuprofen), bandages, a first aid ointment for small cuts, sterile wipes, gauze and

tape, an elastic bandage for a sprain, an insect bite cream, antihistamines, and a sunburn relief cream. Yes, this seems like a lot for a simple day out, but things go wrong, and even if the lifeguard on duty has many of these things in stock, you shouldn't count on it. None of these items will take up much space. Better safe than sorry! There's more on first aid and emergency response in a separate section (see page 58).

FOR ANY MORE SERIOUS INJURIES, CONTACT THE LIFEGUARD RIGHT AWAY, OR MAKE SURE THAT YOU HAVE CELL PHONE RECEPTION TO DIAL FOR HELP. DON'T RISK BEING CAUGHT OUT ALONE!

LEAVE VALUABLES AT HOME. It's just too easy for things to get lost, stolen, or damaged. Ask yourself if you really need your electronic devices. Probably not, except your phone for emergencies. If you must have something else with you, take precautions to make sure that everything is well protected from the elements. Water, sand, and sun can all wreak havoc on sensitive electronics, so be careful about how you use them. For things like wallets, keys, and phones, have a small, waterproof bag that you can store them in. Keep it with you, or with a trusted companion, at all times. Better yet, keep them in a small, waterproof box, a plastic container, or so on. Keep your phone charged at all times, and consider getting a portable charger to keep it topped up.

USE SPEAKERS OR EARBUDS FOR SOME BEACH TUNES. If you want to listen to music, be mindful of your fellow beachgoers. Nobody wants to be serenaded by some obnoxious people blasting their tunes loudly on a speaker, and yet we've probably all had to put up with it. It's very annoying—don't do it. Either keep the volume very low, or wear earbuds. Or better yet, take in the natural sounds around you, enjoy the washing and crashing of the waves, and attune to a different environment. You can listen to music anytime, so try something different by the sea.

BRING A BEACH READ. Consider having some old-fashioned entertainment. If you've swum and run around and are a bit tired but aren't ready to leave yet, a good book can be just the thing. There is a whole culture around beach and summer reading, so why not indulge in it? Bring a new book you've been dying to read and dip into it when you need a break from other activities. A reading tablet is fine if you want a selection of material to browse. It can be great for audio books, if you just want to close your eyes and tune in to an engaging story. But be mindful of the elements; none of these devices take kindly to sand, sun, or water!

BRING STURDY BEACH TOYS FOR KIDS. We'll discuss children specifically in a later entry (see page 98), but as a general guide, bring inflatable beach balls, sandcastle-building buckets and shovels, and so on. You'll want items that will keep them entertained and that will hold up to whatever they put them through! For an infant, a small, inflatable baby pen that is well sheltered against the sun is a must. Be mindful of what activities are permitted at the beach in question, and plan your kids' entertainment according to those rules.

FOOD & DRINK

If you're spending any amount of time at the beach, food and drink are going to be a necessity. Sure, you might be able to go and grab something to eat at a nearby vendor, but a beach picnic is so much more fun! What you decide to bring is ultimately up to your personal tastes, but here are some ideas for foods and accessories that will make your beach picnic the best it can be.

BRING PICNIC BASKETS AND COOLERS.

You don't need to have a classic picnic basket, of course, but you'll want a sturdy, waterproof container that can hold nonperishable foods: crackers, chips, pretzels, nuts, dried fruits, beef jerky, popcorn, cookies, energy bars, snack and party mixes, bread, and whatever else you might like. These containers can be insulated or not, as you need. A cooler should have ice or ice packs so that you can bring drinks, cheeses, meats, green salad, pasta salad, wraps, yogurt, dips (hummus, cheese dips, fresh salsa, guacamole), chocolate (be careful, though, since it can melt and make a mess!), or anything that might be perishable, especially on hot days.

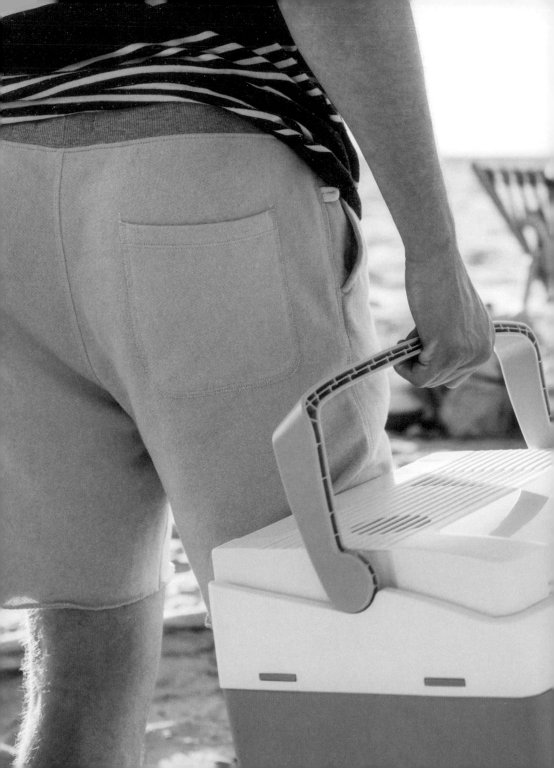

WATER IS ESSENTIAL. Whether you bring your own in thermoses and bottles, or acquire it at the beach, you need to stay hydrated throughout the day. Sodas, iced tea, and juices are also fine, as long as you're still drinking water. If you want to bring alcohol, limit it to lighter beverages like beer and chilled white or rosé wine, which will be more refreshing on a hot day anyway. Boxed wine can be a great choice, as it's far less likely to spill. Try to stay away from spirits and liquor, since their higher alcohol levels are not a good mix with beach weather! Also check to make sure that alcohol is allowed at your beach; not every place permits it.

FRUITS ARE GREAT CHOICES. Strawberries, blueberries, grapes, raspberries, or anything small that can be rinsed and eaten with the skin on is an excellent option. Tangerines and small oranges are good too, if a bit sticky. Be wary of fruit like apples; you'll need to bring them whole and slice them at the beach, since they turn brown pretty quickly once exposed to the air. Bananas have the potential to turn brown and squishy too, so leave them at home.

SMALL VEGGIES CAN BE GREAT SNACKS. Try cherry tomatoes, mini carrots, small cucumbers, celery sticks, sliced mushrooms, bell pepper slices, and so on. These are especially good with dips like hummus, salsa, and cream cheese. Be creative!

BRING FOODS THAT YOUR KIDS WILL LIKE. Splurge and bring their favorites. A beach trip is a fun day out, so it's okay to spoil them a little with some junk foods. Let's be honest—they won't be happy with plates piled with broccoli and green beans!

CONSIDER A PORTABLE GRILL AND CHARCOAL. If the beach allows it and you're up to the task, you might want to bring a portable grill and charcoal, along with tools and foods to grill (burgers, hot dogs, or their vegetarian equivalents). Check to make sure that grilling is permitted first. Some beaches have grills already on-site, which will save you the trouble of hauling your own equipment out there.

NEVER OFFER FOOD TO WILD ANIMALS. That being said, it's probable that a greedy seagull or two will manage to snatch away something of yours before day's end. Perhaps we should say never *willingly* offer food to wild animals!

DON'T FORGET TO BRING DISHES. That includes plates, cups, utensils, napkins, a few small bowls, a platter, and whatever else you might need. These can be reusable plastic (preferable), or disposable, but make sure that you take everything away with you when you leave. On that note...

REMEMBER TO CLEAN UP AFTER YOURSELF. Bring hand wipes, hand sanitizer, paper towels, and bags for trash and/or recycling. Always throw away all trash, recycle what can be recycled, and take everything else home with you.

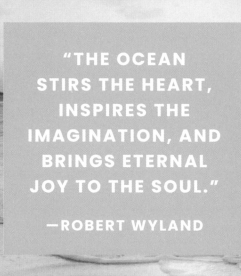

"THE OCEAN
STIRS THE HEART,
INSPIRES THE
IMAGINATION, AND
BRINGS ETERNAL
JOY TO THE SOUL."

—ROBERT WYLAND

THE BEST ARRIVAL TIMES

The best time to arrive at the beach is really up to you, and again, it depends on what you want out of the experience. Some people are morning people; a lot of others aren't. Some people love late nights, while others are passing out by 11:00 p.m. Here are some things to keep in mind.

IF THE WEATHER IS WARM AND THE BEACH IS GOING TO BE CROWDED, you will probably want to get there early to stake out your place ahead of the crowds. There will always be people arriving later, even late in the day, so getting there early ensures that you get the spot you want and don't have to settle for someplace you don't like. You might grumble about having to get up early, but you'll be thankful once you're there!

IF YOU'RE AN EARLY BIRD AND YOUR BEACH FACES THE EAST, there are few things more incredible and beautiful than watching a colorful sunrise over the water, except maybe seeing a sunset over the water! Even if you hate mornings, it's worth giving this a try once just to see it.

IF YOUR GOAL IS TO HAVE A CLASSIC DAY OUT, you'll want to set up early, and then be ready to get on with your favorite activities as soon as you can. That way, if the beach crowds up later, you'll have had the chance to do stuff without so many people getting in your way. Remember to protect yourself during the most intense hours of sunlight: 10:00 a.m. to 4:00 p.m.

IF YOU LIKE LATER TIMES, and especially if your beach faces the west, it can be very rewarding to arrive in the afternoon, after 4:00 p.m. Crowds will be dispersing, and you might well have as much of the beach to yourself as you would have if you'd gotten there early in the day. Also, if you hang around long enough, you might be treated to a spectacular sunset over the waves, assuming your beach faces the west!

IF YOU'RE A NIGHT OWL, and your beach and/or local authorities allow it, the beach can be a great place for an evening gathering. True, you might not be going swimming or surfing (though some experienced people do, even though it's not recommended), but sitting around a fire with friends, cooking food, and sharing laughs and good times can be one of the most enjoyable experiences imaginable. The beach can take on a whole different character at night, and you might even witness a moonrise over the water. Music, food, and maybe even dancing are all fun possibilities for a nighttime romp at the beach.

TIKI COCKTAIL
RECIPES

Some drinks are just made for sipping on the sand. If you're looking to elevate your beach vacation, then these cocktails are for you! Perfect for a girls' trip, beach party, or simple lounge in the sun, your beach cooler is just begging for some summer refreshments. Make sure you stay hydrated and limit your alcohol intake while in the heat. Pack these drinks up in your cooler ahead of time so that you can enjoy them while you relax in the sea breeze.

PLANTER'S PUNCH

GLASSWARE: COLLINS GLASS

GARNISH: EDIBLE ORCHID

---

2 oz. Appleton Estate Reserve Blend rum

½ oz. grenadine

¼ oz. demerara syrup

¼ oz. St. Elizabeth Allspice Dram

½ oz. fresh lime juice

2 dashes Angostura bitters

1 Place all of the ingredients, except for the bitters and edible orchid, in a cocktail shaker, fill it two-thirds of the way with ice, and shake vigorously until chilled.

2 Fill the Collins glass with ice and strain the cocktail over it.

3 Top the cocktail with the bitters, garnish it with the edible orchid, and enjoy.

MAI TAI

GLASSWARE: MAI TAI GLASS

GARNISH: FRESH MINT, SPENT LIME SHELL

2 oz. Appleton Estate Reserve Blend rum

¾ oz. curaçao

½ oz. orgeat

½ oz. fresh lime juice (reserve spent lime shell for garnish)

¼ oz. rock candy syrup

1 Place all of the ingredients, except for the garnishes, in a cocktail shaker, fill it two-thirds of the way with crushed ice, and shake vigorously until chilled.

2 Pour the contents of the shaker into the Mai Tai glass, garnish with the fresh mint and reserved lime shell, and enjoy.

HURRICANE

1 oz. Hamilton Jamaica Black rum

1 oz. Appleton Estate Reserve Blend rum

1¼ oz. passion fruit blend

¼ oz. fresh lemon juice

Dash Peychaud's Bitters

1   Place all of the ingredients, except for the lemon wheel, in a cocktail shaker, fill it two-thirds of the way with crushed ice, and shake vigorously for three times as long as usual.

2   Pour the contents of the shaker into the Hurricane glass, garnish with the lemon wheel, and enjoy.

BLUE HAWAIIAN

¾ oz. vodka

¾ oz. Pusser's Rum

½ oz. blue curaçao

3 oz. pineapple juice

1 oz. sweet & sour mix

1   Place all of the ingredients, except for the dehydrated pineapple slice, in a cocktail shaker, fill it two-thirds of the way with crushed ice, and shake vigorously until chilled.

2   Fill the coupe with crushed ice and strain the cocktail over it.

3   Garnish the cocktail with the dehydrated pineapple slice and enjoy.

THREE DOTS
AND A DASH

GLASSWARE: COLLINS GLASS

GARNISH: 3 LUXARDO MARASCHINO CHERRIES,
PINEAPPLE LEAVES

1½ oz. rhum agricole

½ oz. El Dorado 3-Year rum

¼ oz. St. Elizabeth Allspice Dram

½ oz. falernum

½ oz. honey syrup

½ oz. fresh orange juice

½ oz. fresh lime juice

1   Place all of the ingredients, except for the garnishes, in a cocktail shaker, fill it two-thirds of the way with crushed ice, and shake vigorously until chilled.

2   Fill the Collins glass with ice and strain the cocktail over it.

3   Thread the cherries on a skewer.

4   Garnish the cocktail with the cherries and pineapple leaves and enjoy.

ORIGINAL FROZEN MARGARITA

GLASSWARE: MARGARITA COUPE

GARNISH: LIME WHEEL

2 oz. tequila plata

1½ oz. freshly squeezed lime juice

1 oz. simple syrup

1½ oz. orange liqueur

1 cup ice

Sea salt, for the rim

1　Place all of the ingredients, except for the sea salt and lime wheel, in a blender and blend until there are no large pieces.

2　Rub the lime wheel around the edge of the margarita coupe and dip the rim into the salt. Pour the contents of the blender into the glass, garnish with the lime wheel, and enjoy.

PAINKILLER

2½ oz. Hamilton Guyana 86 rum

1 oz. cream of coconut

1 oz. orange juice

4 oz. pineapple juice

1   Place all of the ingredients, except for the garnishes, in a cocktail shaker, fill it two-thirds of the way with crushed ice, and shake vigorously until chilled.

2   Pour the contents of the shaker into the tiki mug, garnish with the orange slice, cinnamon stick, and freshly grated nutmeg, and enjoy.

CARIBBEAN MILK PUNCH

GLASSWARE: TUMBLER

GARNISH: FRESHLY GRATED NUTMEG

---

1 oz. vanilla syrup

1 oz. Smith & Cross rum

½ oz. bourbon

1 oz. heavy cream

1 Place all of the ingredients, except for the freshly grated nutmeg, in a cocktail shaker, fill it two-thirds of the way with crushed ice, and shake vigorously until chilled.

2 Fill the tumbler with ice and strain the cocktail over it.

3 Garnish the cocktail with the freshly grated nutmeg and enjoy.

PIÑA COLADA

1 oz. white rum

1 oz. coconut milk

1 oz. triple sec

2 oz. pineapple juice

1　Place all of the ingredients, except for the pineapple wedge, in a blender with about ½ cup of crushed ice. Blend until smooth.

2　Pour the contents into the glass, garnish with the pineapple wedge, and enjoy.

TEQUILA SUNRISE

GLASSWARE: HIGHBALL GLASS

GARNISH: MARASCHINO CHERRY, ORANGE SLICE

2 oz. tequila

1 dash lemon juice

4 oz. orange juice

1 splash grenadine

1. Add ice to the highball glass and pour in the tequila and dash of lemon juice.

2. Add the orange juice. Top with the grenadine and allow it to settle. Garnish with the cherry and orange slice and enjoy.

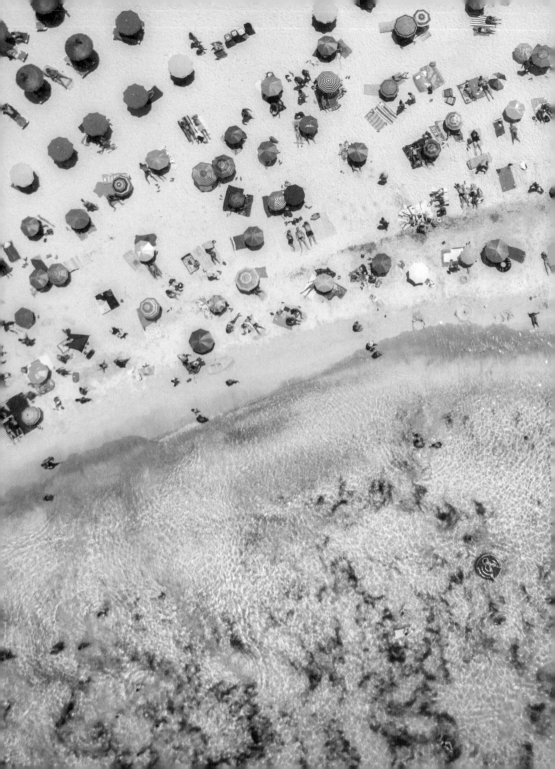

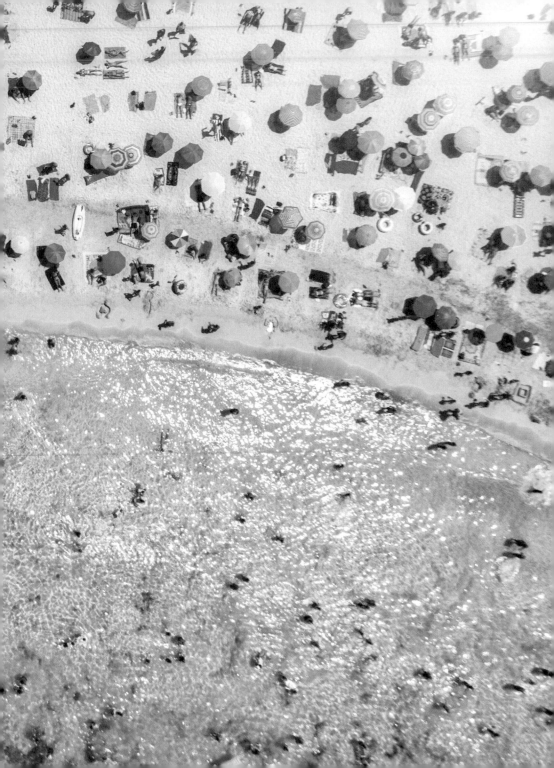

HEALTH & SAFETY

ALL ABOUT LIFEGUARDS

Not every beach has one—and if they don't, they will probably post clear signs saying this—but a lifeguard is very desirable, even essential when planning your day out at the beach. This is especially true if you have children with you. Again, it will largely depend on what activities you have planned. If you're not going in the water at all, you probably don't need to worry about whether there is a lifeguard on duty or not. But if you plan on spending time in the water, the peace of mind of knowing one is nearby is worth it. Here are some things to keep in mind about lifeguards.

YOU'RE SAFER WITH A LIFEGUARD ON DUTY. If a lifeguard is on duty, your chances of drowning are about (wait for it) 1 in 18 million! So, choosing a beach with a qualified lifeguard on duty is a no-brainer.

LIFEGUARDS MUST UNDERGO VARIOUS TRAININGS AND CERTIFICATIONS. If you plan on swimming, you might want to check with your beach to see what qualifications its lifeguards have. At a bare minimum, lifeguards need to be the following: strong swimmers, attentive to their surroundings at all times, able to recognize dangers and those in distress, able to successfully ask people to get out of the water, physically able to remove a distressed person from the water, able

to perform first aid and CPR (and sometimes more advanced techniques), able to control any irresponsible behavior on the beach, and able to get additional help with any of these issues. They also need to be physically fit and capable of swimming certain distances in a given time, as well as running certain distances in a given time. Lifeguards are athletes!

LIFEGUARDS ALSO ENFORCE BEACH RULES. If there are things that are not allowed—such as dune buggies on the beach, jet skis in the water, and so on—good lifeguards will try to stop any rule breaking, calling in authorities if necessary. Respect the rules of the beach and make your lifeguard's job easier!

LIFEGUARDS WORK SHIFTS. They might change out while you're at the beach. This is normal and gives them a chance to take a break. If you're lucky, your beach will have more than one on duty at the same time, especially if the beach is large.

LIFEGUARDS ARE USUALLY NOT PAID ALL THAT MUCH. Be mindful that they are doing a potentially stressful and dangerous job that requires their constant attention. Most are lifeguards because they enjoy being at the beach, enjoy swimming, and enjoy beach culture. Being sociable is part of the job, and most will be happy to answer your questions or help you if they can. But be respectful of their job requirements, responsibilities, and time. And please, don't get angry or mouth off to one of them if they are just doing their job!

ALL ABOUT TIDES

Tides, of course, are the rising and falling of water levels, mainly oceanic, but also (to a much lesser extent) in large lakes. We talk of the tides going in or coming out as they are pulled by the moon and the rotation of the Earth—all very nice and even romantic, but tides are something that you, as a beachgoer, need to be aware of. It's neat to see them go in and out, but they can pose several dangers. Here is some important information.

TIDES CAN VARY WIDELY. Throughout the course of the day, they change as much as 30 feet or more up and down a beach. So, if you are sitting closer to the water, you might find that you need to move back later on when the tide comes in.

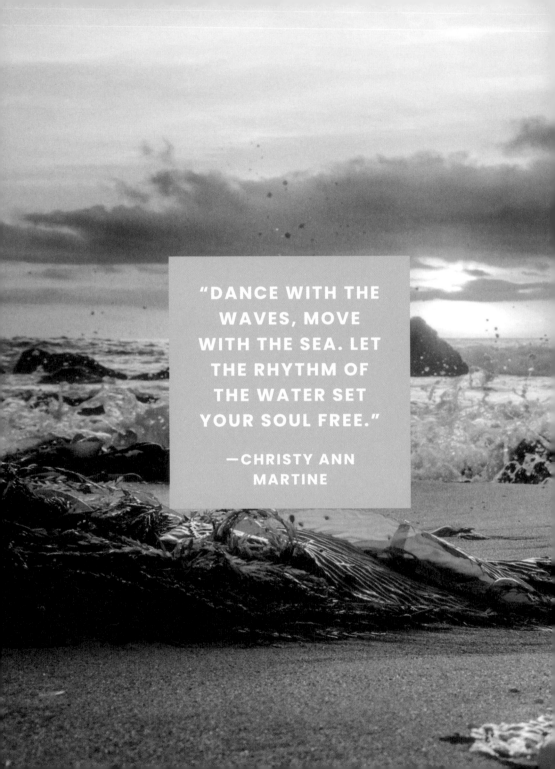

"DANCE WITH THE WAVES, MOVE WITH THE SEA. LET THE RHYTHM OF THE WATER SET YOUR SOUL FREE."

—CHRISTY ANN MARTINE

TIDES ARE AFFECTED BOTH BY GRAVITY AND WEATHER CONDITIONS. Storms can obviously make them more extreme. Tidal surges are more likely with unpredictable weather, but even if your beach is calm, there can be factors out at sea that will affect tidal currents.

WATCH THE DIRECTION OF TIDES. Tides generally come in slowly, but you need to be mindful of them. It's worth learning how to read a tide table, especially one for your area. These tend to be quite accurate and will give you valuable information about tidal movements and how to stay safe.

BE MINDFUL OF WALKING INTO COVES, BAYS, OUTCROPPINGS OF ROCK, OR OTHER AREAS THAT ARE ADJACENT TO THE MAIN BEACH. TIDES CAN COME IN FAIRLY RAPIDLY IN THESE AREAS, AND YOU MIGHT FIND YOURSELF BEING CUT OFF FROM ANY WAY TO RETURN.

CHECK IN WITH YOUR LIFEGUARD. They're a great source for information on tides if you have any concerns. Lifeguards will know about tidal courses and can advise beachgoers if they need to move. Always listen to your lifeguard!

WATCH THE WEATHER. Even though tide tables are a good guide, they can be off if there are strong weather patterns or shifts in the wind. Again, your lifeguard will probably be kept in the know about any unforeseen changes and will be able to advise visitors of what they need to do.

WATCH WHERE YOU WALK. Make sure that you know the times for incoming and outgoing water. Don't explore risky areas alone, and always make sure that someone knows where you are. Keep your phone with you in a waterproof container in case you get into trouble.

ONE OF THE SAFER TIMES TO SWIM IS DURING A "SLACK TIDE." This is about 30 minutes before and after high or low tide. The waves will be calmer and the water will not seem to be rising or falling. This is only a rule of thumb, however, and you must still stay mindful of local conditions and your lifeguard's instructions.

ALL ABOUT TIDAL POOLS

One of the best things about low tide at rocky beach areas is a chance to wander out on the rocks and see the tidal pools teeming with marine life. This excursion can be great fun and educational for you and the little ones, but you must use care and precaution. Here are some guidelines.

ALWAYS WATCH THE TIDES. Never venture out into a tidal pool area without knowing when the tide is going out and coming in. Tide tables will help you determine when tidal pools are exposed and when you can safely walk out to them. They will also tell you when the water is returning. Generally, a good time to set off is about half an hour before low tide, since the water will still be receding. Be careful about how far out you go, however, especially if you have small children with you.

ALWAYS KEEP AN EYE ON ANY CHILDREN WITH YOU. Do not let them wander off alone. Rocks can be slippery, and even at low tide, waves can crash up against the rocks and knock someone off their feet. There is a real danger of being swept away into the ocean. Always face the direction of the ocean (not the shore) and keep an eye on the waves.

WATCH WHERE YOU STEP. Rocks are often covered with seaweed or algae and can be very slippery. This is a danger for both children and adults. You can slip and potentially sprain or even break your wrist or ankle if you're not careful. In addition, rocks can be jagged or covered with shells or barnacles that can cause bad cuts to your hands and arms. Always walk slowly and carefully. Wear good waterproof shoes that cover your feet. Never go out in flip-flops or sandals. Step on the driest places that you can.

CARRY SOMETHING WITH YOU FOR FIRST AID. This is important in case you get cut. If you are bleeding, dry off the wound and bandage it, and keep it out of the water.

REMEMBER THAT YOU ARE ENTERING INTO ANOTHER WORLD. The sea creatures that you might find out there are wild animals, and this is their home. Mind your step so as not to accidentally step on or crush these small animals, and try to observe them from a distance that is safe for them.

NEVER PICK UP SEA CREATURES! If you find crabs, starfish, or any other animals, please leave them alone. Tidal pools are not petting zoos—they're for observation only. Handling creatures can cause them distress and leave them vulnerable to predators if you don't put them back exactly where you found them. Some animals—such as crabs, jellyfish, and sea urchins—will react on instinct to being picked up and go into defense mode, pinching or stinging you, and you'll have no one to blame but yourself.

ALWAYS PICK UP LITTER. Any kind of trash can cause harm to sea creatures, so if you see something lying in a pool or on a rock, by all means, do the right thing and take it with you. Bring a plastic bag with you just in case, and do your part to clean up the ocean and keep it safe for the animals that live in it.

ALL ABOUT SPF

When spending time at the beach, it can't be emphasized enough that you need to protect yourself from the sun, no matter what time of day. While those with darker skin tones have more natural protection, any change in skin color represents at least some damage to your skin. In these small amounts, it won't likely be a concern, but over time, and with constant sun exposure, you run an increasing risk of developing some form of skin cancer. In the United States, skin cancer is the most common form of cancer, and it's estimated that one in five people will develop it during their lifetime. Those are not ideal odds! And remember that you can get sunburned even on a cloudy day. All the more reason you need to take your sunscreen seriously. Here are some tips for staying safe in the sun.

ALWAYS BUY NEW SUNSCREEN AT THE START OF A BEACH SEASON. Don't rely on last year's, even if you have a decent amount left over. The fresher, the better. Make sure you check the expiration date on new sunscreen as well.

USE A SUNSCREEN THAT PROTECTS AGAINST UVA AND UVB. The SPF should be 15 or higher, at the very least. It's better to have a higher number, especially if you will be in the water or outside quite a lot during the day. In that case, start with 30 and go up from there. SPF 50 is also quite reasonable. It never hurts to be cautious!

LATHER UP EARLY. Apply at least one ounce of sunscreen to your body about 30 minutes before going out into the sun. Reapply sunscreen liberally throughout the day, at least once every two hours. A combination of water, sweat, and the elements will weaken and rinse off the sunscreen you're wearing, so frequently slap on more! If you're swimming, try to use a sunscreen that is waterproof, but reapply it when you come out of the water anyway. Remember that water reflects UV rays, so you should use a sunscreen with a minimum SPF of 30 if you're swimming in an ocean or lake.

USE ONE SUNSCREEN FOR YOUR BODY AND A SEPARATE ONE FOR YOUR FACE. You should consider doing this if you are prone to breakouts or other reactions. There are sunscreens specially formulated for the face. Don't forget to cover your lips and any part line you might have in your hair; these areas are particularly vulnerable to burns!

BE MINDFUL OF THE TYPE OF SUNSCREEN YOU ARE USING. Certain sunscreens contain chemicals such as avobenzone, ecamsule, octocrylene, and oxybenzone that are absorbed into the skin and therefore into one's bloodstream. While these sunscreens are generally deemed safe to use, the jury is still out, and some researchers advise caution in using them too much. More studies are needed to determine safety with long-term use.

TRY TO USE "REEF SAFE" SUNSCREENS. These contain only ingredients that are intended to be more environmentally safe, and don't leach any damaging chemicals into the ocean ecosystem. The label will probably indicate if a sunscreen is reef safe or coral safe, but since these terms are not yet regulated, there can still be some doubts about whether a given sunscreen is truly environmentally friendly. If a sunscreen has the "Protect Land + Sea" certification seal, it is safe to use in all water environments. If not, try to find sunscreens without the following ingredients: microplastic spheres or beads, nanoparticles such as zinc oxide or titanium dioxide, oxybenzone, octinoxate, 4-methylbenzylidene camphor, octocrylene, para-aminobenzoic acid (PABA), methylparaben, ethylparaben, propylparaben, butylparaben, benzylparaben, and triclosan. Yes, this is a bit of work, but it's worth it! And it's not just some eco-friendly fad. Since 2018, Hawaii has had a ban on oxybenzone and octinoxate sunscreens, and Aruba, Palau, and Bonaire have now passed their own bans. The Florida Keys also recently passed similar legislation, so you can expect to see more and more eco-sunscreen-only laws showing up.

BE MINDFUL OF YOUR SKIN TYPE.

Remember, the paler or more freckled your skin, the more you are at risk for sunburn. If you want to get that tan without having the sun damage your skin, consider a sunscreen that also has a bronzing feature. Artificial tans have come a long way in recent years; remember when they just turned you orange? Now, you can get a rich tan color without the effort or the harm!

BEACH PESTS

As if sun damage wasn't enough of a problem, you'll probably have to contend with stings and bites. It's almost as if nature doesn't want you at the beach at all! Mosquitoes, ticks, and other creepy-crawlies are just waiting for some tasty human snacks, and what better place than a warm location where people are exposing more of their skin in the open air? It's like an insect buffet! So how can you protect yourself? Here are some suggestions.

DO SOME RESEARCH. Check out the beach and its surroundings to find out what might lie in wait for you. Keep in mind that many beaches have crabs, bees, spiders, and other things that bite. The US Environmental Protection Agency (EPA) has an excellent online guide to insect repellents and how to choose and use them safely. Find it at: epa.gov/insect-repellents

THINK AHEAD. Consider where you'll be and what kind of protection you might need. Tropical areas are more likely to have mosquitoes, while a New England beach with an adjacent woodland could be a fine home to ravenous, bloodthirsty ticks.

CHOOSE WISELY. There are different kinds of repellents, many of which contain a chemical called DEET. DEET, while still approved by the EPA, has

> **WEAR COMFORTABLE SHOES AND CONSIDER WEARING CLOTHING THAT COVERS YOUR LEGS WHEN WALKING TO AND FROM THE BEACH. THIS IS ESPECIALLY TRUE IF YOU HAVE TO WALK THROUGH ANY WILDERNESS OR WOODED AREAS TO GET TO THE SANDS.**

come under scrutiny in recent years. Some people claim that it might be unsafe over long-term use, but studies have not yet confirmed this. An alternative to DEET is picaridin, which is a newer invention that offers the same levels of protection and is also EPA approved. In both cases, a minimum of a 20% concentration should do the trick for keeping the bugs away.

BE VIGILANT. Don't neglect this important safety precaution because you can't be bothered to look it up online or buy the product. Though they are small, biting insects are no joke. They can carry a variety of nasty diseases, such as malaria, West Nile virus, Lyme disease, and other unpleasant infections that you don't want in your life. Chances are you'll be fine, but it's always best to be prepared.

"AFTER A VISIT TO THE BEACH, IT'S HARD TO BELIEVE THAT WE LIVE IN A MATERIAL WORLD."

—PAM SHAW

SHOWERING AFTER A SWIM

It might not seem necessary, but you should always shower off after swimming. If you've been in an ocean, or even a big lake, you will have been exposed to various bacteria and contaminants. The US Centers for Disease Control and Prevention (CDC) estimates that the average person has around 0.14 grams of feces on their body at any given time. Gross, but true! So if you've just been in the water with several dozen other swimmers nearby, guess what's likely floating all around you? Yuck! And if you've had your mouth open and swallowed any seawater? Double yuck! There isn't much you can do about that (except try to keep your mouth shut!). Here are some further thoughts about this whole unpleasant business.

BEWARE OF BACTERIA. Recent studies have shown that swimmers come out of the water with 70% more antibiotic resistance genes (known as ARGs) on their skin after being in the ocean. If swimmers stayed in the water for several hours, the increase could be up 300%! These kinds of numbers mean that you are at an increased risk for skin infections after a long ocean swim. The sooner you rinse off after being out in the waves, the better.

BEWARE OF POLLUTION AND WASTE. The problem is made worse by the fact that human wastewater can find its way into the sea. This water can contain traces of pharmaceuticals, harmful bacteria, and other chemicals that leach out into the ocean. Anyone swimming in these waters can unknowingly expose themselves to harmful levels.

WASH YOURSELF OFF AS SOON AS POSSIBLE. If you come out of the water with fecal bacteria and other unpleasant microorganisms or chemicals on your skin and in your hair, it's a good idea to rinse that all away. Remember, the longer you stay in the water, the more likely you are to be exposed.

USE THE OUTDOOR SHOWERS PROVIDED BY MANY BEACHES. These can give you a quick rinse, though it's good to use some soap too. Keep a simple liquid soap handy that you can use to wash off your body and hair. It doesn't need to be antibacterial and actually shouldn't be, since these products can lead to more bacterial resistance. You also don't need a washcloth or loofah, just use your hands to work up a good lather, and rub your body until you've gotten soap all over it. Obviously, you'll still be wearing swimming clothing (unless you're at a nude beach), so you won't be able to give it as good a wash, but do what you can.

CHECK THE WATER QUALITY BEFORE YOU SWIM. You can probably check the water quality online for any given beach. Do so before you go swimming if you have any concerns about safety.

SAFETY & EMERGENCIES

Generally, beach days are fun for the whole family, and with a little caution and preparation, you'll come home with nothing more than good memories and some cool photos and videos. But there are a number of possible dangers at beaches that you need to be aware of. Some of these are minor and unlikely, but it's best to at least familiarize yourself with them, especially if you will be swimming, snorkeling, or engaging in any other water activities.

DON'T OVERESTIMATE YOUR SWIMMING ABILITIES. You might be a very good swimmer, but remember that even skilled swimmers can get into trouble. If you are inexperienced, but still want to paddle about in the waves closer to shore, make sure that you do so near a lifeguard station, so that you can see them and they can see you at all times.

BEWARE OF RIP CURRENTS. These are strong currents that flow away from the shore and can quickly pull you out to sea without much warning. There might be signs posted that warn you about them, and sometimes you can identify them by seeing different-colored water near the shore. Indeed, they appear most often near the shore and extend out to where surfers like to begin their rides. If you do find yourself caught in one, do not fight against it! Instead, try to swim parallel to the shore and then slowly head back toward land at an angle, not directly toward shore. This will give you the best chance of getting out of it. Rip currents are not caused by bad or even windy weather and can form even on calm days. They are a big reason why you should only swim at beaches with lifeguards, since they account for about 80% of all rescues that lifeguards make. If you are in doubt about rip current activity at your beach, ask your lifeguard!

BEWARE OF SHORE BREAK CONDITIONS. This is a condition where the beach slopes off rapidly into the water, allowing for waves to peak quickly and then break steeply and sharply against the shore, rather than in a more gradual way, as they would on a more gently sloping beach. Shore break is especially a concern for surfers, but it can affect swimmers as well. These kinds of waves can literally throw surfers and swimmers into the air and cause severe injuries to the neck and spinal cord. Again, always check with the beach and the lifeguard about the potential risks from unpredictable waves, and familiarize yourself with wave conditions before venturing out into the water.

WATCH OUT FOR JELLYFISH. Yes, it seems like a cliché, but jellyfish are a genuine issue. These strange, almost alien-like creatures can float majestically and beautifully in the water. They are colonies of life-forms that all have the same protective mechanism: they sting. Most jellyfish have venom that is not harmful to humans. The good news is that only about 70 out of the 2,000 or so known species of jellyfish have venom that can cause pain and worse. The not-so-good news is that of those 70, there are some species that float close enough to shore to be a hazard. Keep an eye out for jellyfish both in the water and on the beach itself; they can still sting on land. If you are stung, don't rinse the sting with water (or pee on it, for goodness' sake!), as this can actually spread the venom around, releasing more. Find your lifeguard for first aid. Seek medical attention if you are having an allergic reaction!

BE MINDFUL OF HARMFUL ALGAL BLOOMS (HABs). Also known as "red tides," these blooms occur in coastal waters at certain times of the year. There are usually reliable forecasts for when such blooms will happen, and it's important for you to know them. This is why shellfish are off the menu at certain times of the year, as they have ingested these blooms, and eating them would be toxic. Some beaches might be closed if a known bloom is happening off the coast. Make sure you check ahead of time so that you don't show up to a closed beach and get turned away, disappointed. Not all blooms are poisonous, but some dangerous blooms can occur that are unknown to the authorities. If you swim in water afflicted by a HAB and you ingest too much of that water, you could be in danger. HABs can be fatal in large enough amounts, so do your research to learn more about HABs in your area.

BE MINDFUL OF OTHER HAZARDOUS CONDITIONS. Sometimes beaches are closed due to contamination in the ocean water—from an oil spill, chemical runoff, excess fertilizer, bacterial growth, and so on. If your favorite beach is closed, never try to defy the order and go anyway! At the very least, you might get arrested if you're found out, and at worst, you could be subjecting yourself to dangerous levels of some substance. As always, do your homework first, and check on conditions before you go. While such closures are relatively rare, you don't want to arrive, only to be turned away.

WHAT ABOUT SHARKS? Thankfully, shark attacks are rare, and fatalities are even more so. Currently the odds of being bitten by a shark are 1 in 3,748,067. So, there's not too much to worry about. Still, in 2021, there were 73 recorded incidents of sharks biting humans, and more than half of all shark attacks in the United States occur off the coasts of Florida. Great white sharks are the biggest culprits (cue the *Jaws* theme), but smaller sharks will sometimes attack when they feel threatened or when they are seriously hungry. Sadly, the bigger danger is that posed by humans to sharks, and many species are facing extinction, owing to their food supplies being wiped out by overfishing. This is one of the main reasons why more sharks are swimming closer to shore; they're simply looking for food. Shark attacks are probably not something you need to worry about too much, but it's worth reading up on the statistics and general safety precautions in your area—unless, of course, you're going swimming in a large lake!

STAYING HYDRATED

The body is made up of 70% water, and if we start losing water from our systems, things can go badly quickly. Dehydration can sneak up on you if you're out enjoying yourself in the sun, especially if you're engaging in a lot of physical activity. The hotter it is, the more you'll sweat, which increases your chances of not retaining enough water in your body. Here are some important tips for keeping yourself well watered at all times.

ALWAYS DRINK WATER FREQUENTLY THROUGHOUT THE DAY. Make sure that everyone with you does too, especially children. A thermos filled with water and ice cubes that can be refilled is ideal. Get one with a tight, sealable lid so you can drink water frequently all day.

BE MINDFUL OF HOW MUCH ACTIVITY YOU ENGAGE IN. This is especially true if it's hot outside. We sweat to cool our bodies, but if we don't replenish ourselves with enough water, we can lose the ability to regulate our core temperatures. This in turn makes us overheat and can quickly lead to health problems. Also, we need more water as we age, since our bodies will get to a higher temperature before we start sweating.

LEARN THE DIFFERENT KINDS OF HEAT-RELATED ILLNESSES. If you experience any of these symptoms, stop what you are doing, drink water, and seek immediate assistance: muscle cramps in the calves, quads, and abs. These muscles might feel hard to the touch, but you might not yet feel overheated. The next stage is heat exhaustion. Your core temperature will be higher, at least 101°F (38.3°C), and you will probably have some of the following: headache, nausea, vomiting, feeling faint and weak, and cold or clammy skin. Heat exhaustion can worsen and become heatstroke. Heatstroke is an emergency that happens when your body reaches the temperature of 104°F (40°C). You might feel hot, but your body will no longer sweat. This is an emergency and requires immediate medical attention. Untreated heatstroke can lead to brain damage, organ failure, and death. Your lifeguard will be able to help.

AVOID OR LIMIT ALCOHOL. You might love the taste, but alcohol can lead to quicker dehydration. Alcohol suppresses a hormone in your body that assists in retaining water. If you're out in the heat and knocking back the beers, you might be getting dehydrated more quickly than you would otherwise. Even if you don't get dehydrated, you might face other dangers; being drunk and trying to swim in an ocean or lake definitely do not mix! And there's always the risk of a hangover the next day, which can be a bummer if you're on vacation.

KEEP AN EYE ON THE HEAT INDEX FOR THE DAY. Sometimes, it really is just too hot and humid outside, no matter how much time you intend to spend in the water or how much water you drink. It's okay to give the beach a miss and do something else.

IF YOU DO PLAN TO DRINK ALCOHOL, HAVE A FULL SERVING OR MORE OF WATER WITH EACH DRINK, AND MAKE SURE TO EAT BEFORE OR DURING YOUR DRINKING. THIS WILL HELP SLOW ABSORPTION. ALSO, HAVE NO MORE THAN ONE ALCOHOLIC DRINK PER HOUR, AND LIMIT YOUR OVERALL INTAKE TO TWO DRINKS IN THE DAY.

"LIVE IN THE SUNSHINE, SWIM THE SEA, DRINK THE WILD AIR."

—RALPH WALDO EMERSON

FUN IN THE SUN

JUST FOR KIDS

Beach trips are practically made for children, and can be a highlight of their summer vacations. Your kids will be only too happy to plan out their days with numerous activities that will leave you feeling run ragged and exhausted. But with a little careful planning, you can set up a day of fun that will make everyone happy.

REMEMBER THAT NOT EVERY BEACH ALLOWS EVERY ACTIVITY. Be sure there are enough things to do that your kids won't get bored or frustrated. Happily running on the sand and splashing in the water can keep most kids entertained for a very long time, so there's often no need for elaborate entertainments. In this case, simpler really is better.

ALWAYS KEEP AN EYE ON CHILDREN. This is especially true if they are playing in or near the water.

SUNSCREEN IS VERY IMPORTANT FOR CHILDREN, especially babies and toddlers, whose sensitive skin is more susceptible to the sun's rays. You'll want to make sure that you apply sunscreen to your kids often throughout the day, even if they protest. Most of us can remember getting at least one bad sunburn as a child, and we should be eager to make sure our own kids don't have to go through that!

PLAN FUN ACTIVITIES. There are an endless number of games and things that can keep your kids happy for hours: relay races, volleyball, soccer, Frisbee, kite flying, tug-of-war, scavenger hunts, building sand-castles, hopscotch and tic-tac-toe with the boards drawn in the sand, making sand angels, or musical towels (just like musical chairs). The mind boggles at the possibilities! Go for educational walks and teach your children about the local ecosystem and wildlife. See what they can spot: crabs, seagulls, seals, and much more. There's no reason any child should ever get bored at the beach.

TEACH YOUR KIDS ABOUT RESPECTING NATURE. Make sure that they understand and participate in cleaning up at the end of the day, taking away everything with them. Good stewardship of the oceans and beaches has to start with the young! In fact, you can make an activity out of it. Take your kids on a hunt for litter to pick up any small items you find, placing them in plastic bags that you bring along with you. This can also be a great educational activity for days when you might not have a lot of time to spend at a beach, or when the weather is colder. A beach day dedicated to cleaning up litter can be a great activity to get children involved in keeping your local beaches clean and safe. Always supervise and make sure that they aren't handling anything dangerous, such as broken glass, sharp lids, and so on.

BUILDING AWESOME SANDCASTLES

A day at the beach makes building a sandcastle or two a necessity. Sandcastles are for everyone, not just children, and if you've ever seen some of the incredible creations made by true artists, you know that sand can be made into dazzling sculptures. Pretty much everyone knows that to make a classic sandcastle, you take wet sand and stack it up with the help of a bucket and tools, but here are some tips to help you and your kids make memorable constructions that stand out.

REMEMBER THAT BUILDING A SANDCASTLE IS SUPPOSED TO BE FUN. It's not a competition, so don't force yourself or your kids to try harder than any of you are willing to. If you're not enjoying it, you're doing it wrong!

YOU WON'T NEED MUCH. Just use sand and water (obviously!); a few simple tools, like a bucket or two (the bigger the better!); and some plastic tools for digging (a shovel is essential) and carving your sand. You can use your bare hands, of course, but having a few tools will make the process easier and more fun.

MIND THE TIDES. Choose a spot above the high tide waterline if you want your sculpture to last a bit longer. If you're going to be putting all this work into it, at least let it be around long enough for you to appreciate it! If it's too close to the water, when the tide rushes in it will destroy all your hard work—unless that's what you want, in which case, go for it!

YOUR SAND HAS TO BE WET ENOUGH TO HOLD A SHAPE. If it isn't, the whole thing will just collapse before you even start. About one part sand to one part water should do the trick.

PACK YOUR WET SAND DOWN TO MAKE IT DENSE. This makes it easier to stack and carve. Be sure to leave room for the water to drain off a bit at the bottom. Don't just fill your bucket with very wet sand, or it might stay stuck in there. Make sure you pound down your wet sand to help form the structures you want. It will stick together well if it's wet enough.

USE THE "VOLCANO METHOD" AS A STARTING POINT. Create a "moat" by digging a circle around your work area, and add sand to make a volcano-ish mound in the middle. Pour a bucket of water into it and push and stomp on the sand to get the water in. This will compact the sand and help it set and keep its shape, kind of like cement. Keep on building up this base as you add more water. Remember, it should be about half and half.

BUILD YOUR WET SANDCASTLE ON THIS MOUND. Take nice globs of wet sand and pack them on. One good idea is to stack your sand in rounded layers (almost like pancakes), which will give it more strength and help you make taller towers. Shape these towers with your hands initially; you can add more detail later on. Keep adding more water as needed. The wetter the structure, the longer it will last. With practice, you can build up some pretty tall towers this way. But be aware that gravity will eventually take its toll, and if you make your structures too tall, at some point they will collapse. Don't keep building up the same tower if it starts getting wobbly.

SHAPE IT! When your sand is good and packed, you can begin to shape it properly and sculpt patterns and designs into it. Again, you'll need to have pretty damp sand so that you can carve away bits and not have it fall over. This might take some experimenting and practice. Small items like spoons and even pencils can help you get the level of detail you want, such as windows, brick patterns, vines, and so on. Artists sometimes use knives and sculpting tools, but with kids around, it's better to limit your tools to unsharp items.

START BUILDING! Build walls the same way you build towers, only instead of making the layers round, make them in brick-like shapes so that you can fashion a wall. Walls won't be as stable as towers and can easily fall over if they're too thin. If you can keep one standing, you can experiment with carving designs on it, or even cutting an arch or doorway into it (be careful, though!). Building a wall between two towers that are close together will give it more stability, so maybe start out with that idea and see how it goes.

BE STRATEGIC. When carving patterns, start at the top and work down, so that loose sand falls over areas you've not worked on yet.

DON'T CARVE TOO DEEPLY. If you do, you could weaken the structure. Keep it light and use long strokes. You don't want to knock over half your tower because you carved too deeply into it. Remember that once you've carved out sand, it's very difficult, if not impossible, to put it back in.

ALL OF THESE TIPS ARE JUST SUGGESTIONS. If you have very young children with short attention spans, or just want to do something quick and fun, then by all means make your castle however you'd like. Just stack up some wet sand and let the ocean knock it over when it comes in. The main goal is to have fun!

TIPS FOR THE BEST SNORKELING

If snorkeling is allowed at the beach you'll be visiting, and you're up for it, you're in for a real treat! It's a chance to see marine life up close and personal and to experience the true beauty of the ocean. Areas like the Caribbean and Hawaii are famous for their dazzling underwater panoramas. If you're a good swimmer, you already have an advantage, but if you've never snorkeled, here are some tips to get you started.

MAKE SURE YOU HAVE GOOD EQUIPMENT. This is the case whether you're renting or buying. Poorly fitting masks will fog up or fill with water and make your experience unpleasant at the very least. Learn how to fit a mask properly. It should be snug, even a bit tight, but not uncomfortable. If you come out of the water with a headache, you've done it wrong!

USE A DRY SNORKEL, OR ONE WITH A SPLASH GUARD. These snorkels have a valve on the top that seals shut when you are underwater, such as when a wave washes over you, or you dive deeper. This will prevent a surge of water from coming down the tube, which is never fun!

MAKE SURE YOUR FINS FIT. Just as important as what goes on your face is what goes on your feet. Fins shouldn't be loose, but they shouldn't be too tight either. When your feet are wet, they will shrink just a bit, so you might need to use fins that seem a bit tight on your dry feet. Fins are essential, so don't skimp on them or avoid them. They provide you with extra force when swimming and will keep you from getting tired out.

MAKE SURE YOU HAVE PRACTICED USING YOUR EQUIPMENT FIRST. This is the case whether you're renting it or buying it. You don't want to get out in the water for real and find that things don't fit right or they feel off. Try practicing in a pool or very shallow body of water first to get a sense of what it's like. Get used to the feel of the snorkel and blowing water out of it. Try out the fins and see how they feel. Keep relaxed at all times. If you're not a confident swimmer, use a flotation vest or other device. Safety first!

DON'T OVEREXERT YOURSELF IN THE WATER. Stay calm and relaxed so that you don't tire out. Float and use your fins to save your energy. Be mindful of currents and tides.

KNOW YOUR EXPERTISE. If you've never snorkeled before, choose a safe and calm place to try it out, and always go with more experienced snorkelers. Mornings are often the best time to go. It's better to wade in from a beach

than go out on a boat and dive into deeper water—
wait until you get better and more confident. Try to
go somewhere that has abundant sea life and beauty;
you want your first time to be memorable! Taking a
beginners' class might be just the thing to ensure that all
of these conditions are met.

**REMEMBER THAT YOU ARE A VISITOR TO
ANOTHER WORLD.** Respect everything around
you; you are only observing it. Only touch rocks and
sand if you need to. Take nothing, disturb nothing, wear
only sunscreen that is reef and coral safe, and, as always,
leave the area as you found it.

**ABOVE ALL, LEARN TO RELAX AND TAKE IN
WHAT YOU SEE.** This is not a competitive sport,
but a chance to commune with some truly wondrous
wildlife and appreciate the ocean's endless beauty.

THE BEST SURFING LOCATIONS

If you're into surfing, you probably already have a pretty good idea of what the best beaches for the sport are, and your list might be very different from someone else's. It all comes down to personal preference and what kind of surfing you like to do. No list can be complete—there are websites that list 50 or even 100 of the best surfing beaches—so the following is just a tiny selection of some great regions around the world that have become classics for surfers. We'll stick to broader areas, rather than specific beaches, so that you have the opportunity to choose what's right for you. Many offer a range of options, from beaches for beginners all the way up to those suitable for advanced surfers. Most of these choices are for warmer-weather surfing, but colder regions can offer their own challenges and rewards.

We're assuming that you already have some surfing experience and know the lingo. If you're a complete beginner, this section won't be as helpful for you; however, if any of these areas appeal to you, read up on them and see what your options are for learning the sport. Many of them have areas that are perfect for beginners. If you do have surfing experience, you'll no doubt make your own bucket list, so look into these places if you're interested. In no particular order:

GOLD COAST, AUSTRALIA

Queensland is the main city along Australia's famed Gold Coast, and it draws surfers from all over the world. Its warm weather and subtropical climate make it an attractive option for surfers, and the best surfing can be had between January and July. It has long beach breaks and an artificial reef at Narrowneck. Beyond Queensland lies some amazing natural beauty, making this an ideal vacation spot.

BUKIT PENINSULA, BALI, INDONESIA

The Bukit Peninsula has attractive surfing options for surfers of every skill level, especially on the northwest coast. There is also some amazing natural beauty to marvel at, as well as the famed eleventh-century Hindu Uluwatu Temple. This region is especially popular with Australian surfers, but it also attracts eager surfers from all over the world, many of whom see it as a bucket list location.

JEFFREYS BAY, SOUTH AFRICA

"J-bay" is the premier location for South African surfers, though it also draws enthusiasts from all over the globe. It's said to have some of the world's best right point breaks (at Supertubes), and has 10 different sections to choose from, depending on your skill level. It's also a popular destination for longboarders and kitesurfers. The water is colder here, and sharks do roam in and out, so be careful and mind the strong currents.

HOSSEGOR, FRANCE

France offers more than fine wine, great cheese, Parisian charm, and Mediterranean fun in the sun. It also has a world-famous surfing area, Hossegor, facing the Atlantic Ocean. It has miles of beach breaks, and some of its features compare favorably to Hawaii, leading many to call it the surfing capital of Europe. It's a bit of a mecca for the rich and famous, and their mansions dot the hills above the beaches, but all are welcome.

PUERTO ESCONDIDO, MEXICO

The "Mexican Pipeline" in Oaxaca is said to have some of the best beach breaks in the world. It's currently an inexpensive getaway where you can rent a beach bungalow and be ready to head right off to the waves. The area boasts beginner-friendly waves as well as challenges for more experienced surfers. Surfing is good for most of the year, with only January and February being the off months. You can also spread out from here and explore other beaches nearby.

SANTA CRUZ, CALIFORNIA

Santa Cruz is famous for its laid-back lifestyle and hippie holdover culture, even as it has gotten more expensive and gentrified in recent years. Fortunately, the surfing is still great— legendary, even—and is suitable for all levels. The city is also home to the famed beach boardwalk, which is sadly now a bit of a ghost of what it used to be, but still worth visiting. Day trips down to Monterey and up to San Francisco are also a must.

RINCON, SANTA BARBARA, CALIFORNIA

There is also a Rincón, Puerto Rico, which has its own surfing culture and charms. Rincon, California, is known as the "Queen of the Coast" and features some of California's best surfing, according to those in the know. It offers a classic point break, one of the best in the world, and is another pilgrimage site for surfers who want to try out all the best locations. It has three main areas and is best for intermediate to advanced surfers. The only problem is that it is right off a main highway and can get very crowded, so plan accordingly.

MALIBU, CALIFORNIA

Malibu needs no introduction. It is home to the first World Surfing Reserve, and its beaches are world-famous, appearing in countless films and television shows. Malibu is arguably *the* stereotypical Southern California beach town, evoking pleasant images of *Baywatch* in many people's minds (though much of that show was filmed a little farther south at Will Rogers State Beach). While there can be as many as 300 surfing-friendly days a year there, bear in mind that it's popular and crowded as a result. Still, if you're serious about the sport, visiting here is a must, since it's the first place in the world where surfing became popular outside of its Hawaiian places of origin.

O'AHU, HAWAII

O'ahu might be the best location of all, being the birthplace of modern surfing as we know it. Some websites simply state that the entire island is excellent for surfing, and leave it at that! CNN listed O'ahu's Pipeline as the world's best surfing spot, even though it's for advanced surfers. Those that surf it say that there's nothing quite like it anywhere else, so that's something to aspire to! On the other hand, beginners do well on the gentler waves at Waikiki. And, of course, the North Shore stretches for 7 miles. As for the best times of year, it's reported that experienced surfers will get the most out of the winter months, while newcomers will enjoy spring better. Whatever your level, there is something at O'ahu that is right for you!

GREAT BEACH TUNES

Everyone has their own specific musical tastes, so if you decide to bring music to the beach, you'll no doubt have some of your own favorites. Unless you've rented a portion of the beach for a private party, you'll not likely be playing music out loud, which would just annoy everyone around you. If you do have the chance to play music on a speaker or smartphone, then your choices will probably reflect the kind of atmosphere of your gathering. You might want straight-up party and dance tunes, or your soundtrack might be more subdued. Pick your favorites. But in the spirit of beach fun, here is a list of 20 classic beach-themed songs that would go well in almost any sun-and-sand setting, even if it's just in the privacy of your own earbuds.

"Under the Boardwalk": The Drifters

"Surf City": Jan & Dean

"Kokomo": The Beach Boys

"Surfin' Safari": The Beach Boys

"Good Vibrations": The Beach Boys

"Surfin' USA": The Beach Boys

"California Girls": The Beach Boys

"(Sittin' On) the Dock of the Bay": Otis Redding

"Wipe Out": The Surfaris

"The Girl from Ipanema": Stan Getz and Astrud Gilberto

"Cruisin'": Smokey Robinson

"In the Summertime": Mungo Jerry

"Itsy Bitsy Teenie Weenie Yellow Polkadot Bikini": Brian Hyland

"Margaritaville": Jimmy Buffett

"One Love": Bob Marley & The Wailers

"Escape (The Piña Colada Song)": Rupert Holmes

"The Boys of Summer": Don Henley

"Walking on Sunshine": Katrina And The Waves

"Island in the Sun": Weezer

"Soak Up the Sun": Sheryl Crow

As you can see, The Beach Boys basically rule beach soundtracks almost by default. There are countless more, of course, so dive into some internet lists of the best beach tunes and pick the ones you like best!

"AT THE BEACH, LIFE IS DIFFERENT. TIME DOESN'T MOVE HOUR TO HOUR BUT MOOD TO MOMENT. WE LIVE BY THE CURRENTS, PLAN BY THE TIDES, AND FOLLOW THE SUN."

—SANDY GINGRAS

WINTER & COLDER-WEATHER ACTIVITIES

While the idea of a beach tends to conjure up thoughts of hot summer days in tropical locations, there is much to be said for beach trips in winter—or at least when the weather is too cold to swim or sit comfortably. If you are a fan of the ocean, there are activities to enjoy all year round. The drama of a seascape seen in winter can be breathtaking, especially if you're visiting a beach in a more northern location. What can you do when it's way too cold to go for a dip? Plenty!

MAKE A FIRE. Not every beach allows fires, but if yours does, then take advantage and get a good one roaring! It will be a great way to keep warm while you're out in the elements, and give you a lovely place to sit, enjoy food and hot drinks, talk, laugh, and pass the time.

HAVE A PICNIC. Food is a must when going to the beach at any time of year. You can tailor your foods to the kind of weather. Instead of ice cream and cold water, enjoy hot coffee or tea, hot chocolate, and cold-weather foods. If you can make a fire, try roasting hot dogs or other foods over it. Bring containers with hot soup or chili. Make sure you have plenty of warm blankets, bring some portable chairs, and have a great afternoon!

BUILD SANDCASTLES—OR SNOW CASTLES! Just because it's cold doesn't mean you can't make a sandcastle or two. The same instructions apply in cold weather, though be mindful of the cold ocean water. And if it has snowed at the beach, make a snow castle instead! It's like a snowman, only it's a castle.

EXPLORE TIDAL POOLS. Cold and overcast weather can be a great opportunity to explore the tide pools, just as in hot weather. There are as many amazing creatures in them in winter as in summer. And again, the same rules apply. Be very careful, never go alone, watch out for slippery places, never leave children unattended, and keep an eye on the tide.

GO FOR A WALK OR HIKE. A walk along the ocean in cold, windy weather can be a dramatic and very satisfying experience. You'll get a real sense of the power of nature, watching the waves crash as the winter winds blow them ashore. If you'd rather not spend too much time along the water itself, colder weather can be a great chance to go for a hike in the surrounding countryside. Try to pick a location where you can hike up a hill to get great views of the beach and the nearby landscape.

FLY A KITE. Windy beaches can be wonderful for kite flying, and you might find that there are already several kite enthusiasts at your beach. Some kite enthusiasts take their hobby very seriously and have the most advanced kites, while others just want to watch a kite flap about in the breeze. Wherever you fall on that spectrum, a windy winter day at the beach can be a perfect spot to get your kite on!

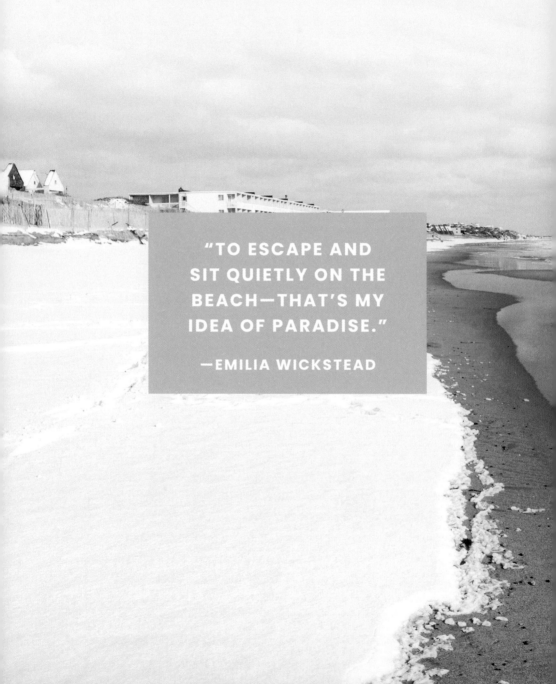

"TO ESCAPE AND SIT QUIETLY ON THE BEACH—THAT'S MY IDEA OF PARADISE."

—EMILIA WICKSTEAD

LOOK FOR SEA LIFE. Winter months can be the time when you have a good chance of spotting migrating whales, or other animals such as seals and otters. If you know that seasonal wildlife might be in your area, bring a pair of binoculars and enjoy the show. Check your local region and see what kind of wild activity there might be.

TAKE PICTURES AND VIDEOS. Wintery days at the beach can offer a great chance to get some memorable photos. Whether capturing waves in the wind and the pelting rain, catching sight of a whale or a flock of migrating birds, or witnessing a stunning winter sunset, you might have many chances to take in the beauty of nature. Go for a good wander and see what comes up.

TAKE A DIP IN A HOT TUB OR HEATED OUT-DOOR POOL. Some hotels and B&Bs have heated outdoor pools or hot tubs that allow you to relax in hot, soothing water, while still taking in the beauty of a wintery beach. Sitting in warm water while it's snowing can be quite the experience!

MAKE SURE YOU BRING THE RIGHT THINGS WITH YOU. Going to the beach in winter is pretty much the opposite of a summer trip. You'll want to bring clothing in layers, windbreakers with hoods in case it rains or snows, warm blankets (fleece is good and lightweight), comfortable seating (such as beach chairs), fire-making tools (if allowed), and the usual selection of waterproof containers, trash bags, and so on. Make sure to check the weather forecast, especially if the weather is changeable. And be mindful of any warnings about unsafe conditions, high tides, water surges, and no-go areas. Play it safe, and you can have just as much fun on a winter beach trip as on a summer one!

NUDE BEACHES

There are nude beaches in many areas of the world, and they might offer a temptation if you're feeling daring, or if you want to get all-over sun exposure—be mindful of how much that could hurt, though! Some beaches are clothing optional, meaning you can get naked if you want, but don't have to, while others are strictly no clothing at all. Decide which option you prefer.

You might think that most nude beaches are hidden away and limited to the very warm parts of the planet, but not all of them are that secluded. These kinds of beaches can be found in a wide variety of regions. There's a nude beach near San Francisco, for example, and if you've ever been to San Fran in the summer, you know that with all the fog, it's not exactly the hottest place to be in July or August. In any case, if you've plucked up your courage and you're a first-timer to a nude beach, here are some important tips and etiquette rules to remember.

FAMILIARIZE YOURSELF WITH LOCAL REGULATIONS AND LAWS. There might be only a part of the beach set aside for nude sunbathers, and you don't want to stroll into a nonnude section and get stared at. Some places only allow partial nudity, or they're topless for women. Make sure you know which kind of beach you're going to.

DON'T STARE OR OGLE. You're not there to see naked people. Obviously, it's inevitable that you will, but respect the fact that others are there to enjoy themselves, just as you are. And it should also go without saying that cameras are absolutely forbidden. Remember that you are going to see all types of bodies at a nude beach: old and young, skinny and not so skinny. Don't go expecting a parade of beach beauties and hunks, or you'll be very disappointed. Be willing to accept others as they are and let them enjoy their day.

BRING A TOWEL. You'll probably be required to always have a towel with you to use when sitting on outdoor furniture. This is a basic health and safety precaution.

TRY NOT TO SIT TOO NEAR TO ANYONE ELSE. Respect their privacy, just as you want them to respect yours. Don't make anyone feel uncomfortable by parking yourself too close. Think about how you'd feel if a naked stranger just flopped right down next to you!

APPLY SUNSCREEN FREQUENTLY AND LIBERALLY. Even more than you might otherwise! You really don't want sunburned private parts. You just don't.

MOST OF THESE BEACHES ARE MORE PRIVATE. This means that many won't have the same amenities as a regular beach might have, so plan accordingly. A lifeguard is still a desirable feature, however.

> **"I COULD NEVER STAY LONG ENOUGH ON THE SHORE; THE TANG OF THE UNTAINTED, FRESH, AND FREE SEA AIR WAS LIKE A COOL, QUIETING THOUGHT."**
>
> **—HELEN KELLER**

"A BEACH IS NOT ONLY
A SWEEP OF SAND,
BUT SHELLS OF SEA
CREATURES, THE SEA
GLASS, THE SEAWEED,
THE INCONGRUOUS
OBJECTS WASHED UP
BY THE OCEAN."

—HENRY GRUNWALD

ARE YOU SHORE WE
HAVE TO LEAVE?

PACKING UP & LEAVING

You've had a great day out, and it's time to pack up and go. What are some of the basic rules about exiting the beach?

TAKE EVERYTHING YOU BROUGHT WITH YOU. If you've generated any garbage or recycling, you must throw it away in the appropriate bins or take it back to the parking lot and dispose of it there. Always check to make sure you haven't left anything behind. Small items like bottle caps and lids can be easy to miss.

CLEAN UP ANY HAZARDS. In general, you shouldn't bring glass products to a beach, since there is a chance they can get broken and leave dangerous shards in the sand that are unseen until someone else steps on them. Even if you think you've cleaned up every piece from a broken glass mishap, chances are you'll miss at least a small piece or two.

HELP KEEP YOUR BEACHES CLEAN. If you see any other garbage left behind by others, pick it up and dispose of it. For sanitary reasons, use plastic bags to pick up any refuse, just as you would when cleaning up after your dog. No, you didn't make the mess and it's technically not your problem, but it's the right thing to do. We all have a responsibility to keep our beaches clean and safe.

BE RESPECTFUL. If the garbage is too much, not safe, or is simply disgusting, alert a lifeguard or other beach authority, so that they can arrange proper pickup.

DOWNLOAD THE NOAA MARINE DEBRIS PROGRAM'S MARINE DEBRIS TRACKER APP. This app can help scientists track the locations of debris. If you really want to help, you can also get involved with the Marine Debris Monitoring and Assessment Project: marinedebris.noaa.gov

FOLLOW THE BASIC RULE OF GOOD BEACH ETIQUETTE: ALWAYS LEAVE EVERYTHING AS YOU FOUND IT!

SOUVENIRS

When you're out at a beach, you'll find yourself surrounded by all sorts of weird and wonderful natural items—things that have washed up onshore or been blown in by the wind. You'll find wood, rocks, shells, and much more. It might be tempting to collect some of these as souvenirs of your trip, especially if you are visiting a faraway place. But should you do it? The answer really depends on what it is and the context. In general, taking items is not a great idea, and it's best to leave the beach as you found it, but here are some thoughts.

DON'T TAKE HOME SAND. Obviously, you'll get a little bit of sand in your shoes and clothes, but some people like to collect a small (or not so small) bag or bottle of the local sand to take home with them and put on display as a reminder of their beach vacation. In short, don't. It disrupts the environment, and in many places around the world, it's illegal. The island of Sardinia, for example, can sentence violators to actual prison time (even years!) for removing its famed white sand. The Greek island of Crete had issues with tourists helping themselves to a local pink sand, so the government designated the area a nature reserve so that no one could go on it. A few selfish individuals ruined it for everyone else, and now the beach is less pink than it used to be. Certain beaches in Hawaii will fine thieves up to $100,000 for sand swiping! Also, never take away any volcanic rocks from Hawaii, whether at the beach or not. There are countless stories of people doing so, only to mail them back because of all the bad luck they bring. You might scoff at this as silly superstition, but the enormous piles of returned rocks featured at some hotels don't lie!

SAND THEFT IS A BIG, UNDERGROUND, CRIMINAL BUSINESS. Sand is used in everything from beauty products to concrete, and there are shady companies that are more than willing to resort to stealing it to get what they need. The world uses something like 50 billion tons of sand per year, and we are using it up faster than the world can replenish it. This is obviously a serious problem, so don't contribute to it by taking sand you don't need from the beaches you visit.

THE BEACH IS NOT A PET STORE. If you are wandering on a beach or near tidal pools, never take away live animals such as hermit crabs or starfish. These are wild creatures and need to be left alone. They will likely not survive in any other environment. If you do happen to find an animal that's injured or in distress, such as a bird or seal, tell your lifeguard immediately, and let them call the proper authorities to deal with it.

WHAT ABOUT SEASHELLS? She might sell seashells by the seashore, but in practice, this is a terrible business to be in. Now, almost everyone has collected a shell or two from the beach, but you might want to reconsider doing this on your next beach visit. Shells of all kinds provide shelter and protection for countless small sea creatures, such as hermit crabs, small fish, and even octopuses. While taking one small shell might not seem like a big deal, if everyone does it, the numbers add up quickly. You should avoid the larger shells you see sometimes for sale, as these have been taken away from living creatures that use them, and those animals are often killed to obtain them. Again, there is an illegal trade in shells that causes devastation to local wildlife populations. Say no to conch shells and other large shells. One study in Spain showed a correlation between an increase in tourism and a decrease in the number of shells on its beaches. Shells help the local ecology and should be left alone.

WHAT ABOUT DRIFTWOOD? You might find a cool-looking piece of wood washed up on a beach that is just lying there, not doing anything. And in most cases, taking it has less of an impact on the environment (though not always). However, on public beaches, driftwood is often not just up for grabs. You might be allowed to take some, but you might need a permit from a local authority to do so, and you could face fines if you don't go through the process. Artists sometimes use driftwood in their work, and this can be fine if they jump through the hoops to obtain it legally. There might be some places where taking driftwood is not allowed. Always check first before helping yourself.

IN SHORT, THE BEST THING TO TAKE AT BEACHES IS PHOTOGRAPHS. Leave the environment as you found it, respect the local ecology, and you'll have just as rewarding an experience—even more so, because you've contributed to keeping the beach a safe and healthy place for all its visitors, human and otherwise!

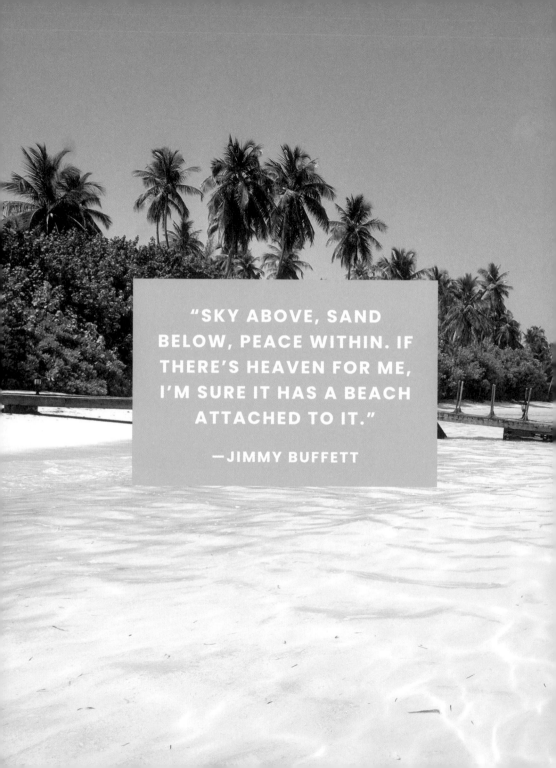

"SKY ABOVE, SAND BELOW, PEACE WITHIN. IF THERE'S HEAVEN FOR ME, I'M SURE IT HAS A BEACH ATTACHED TO IT."

—JIMMY BUFFETT

ONLINE
RESOURCES

Here are a few websites that can be helpful in planning your beach trip, checking on status and safety, or learning more about beach and water activities at a given location.

BEACHMETER.COM

A great all-purpose site with information about beaches, travel, the best vacations spots, and much more.

FREEFUNGUIDES.COM/ BEACH-VACATIONS

Recommendations for hundreds of beaches all around the world.

BEACHTOMATO.COM

Everything beach related, and more!

THESWIMGUIDE.ORG

A great way to find out about the status and conditions of beaches in your area and beyond.

BLUEFLAG.GLOBAL

From the website: The iconic Blue Flag is one of the world's most recognized voluntary awards for beaches, marinas, and sustainable boating tourism operators. To qualify for the Blue Flag, a series of stringent environmental, educational, safety, and accessibility criteria must be met and maintained.

EPA.GOV/BEACH-TECH

Information about American beaches, beach quality, water safety, and other related topics.

EPA.GOV/BEACHES/FIND-IN-FORMATION-ABOUT-PARTICU-LAR-US-BEACH

The title says it all. Look up what you want to know.

WEATHER.GOV/SAFETY/BEACH-RESOURCES

Another site devoted to beach safety and weather information.

ABOUT CIDER MILL PRESS BOOK PUBLISHERS

Good ideas ripen with time. From seed to harvest, Cider Mill Press brings fine reading, information, and entertainment together between the covers of its creatively crafted books. Our Cider Mill bears fruit twice a year, publishing a new crop of titles each spring and fall.

"Where Good Books Are Ready for Press"

501 Nelson Place
Nashville, TN 37214

cidermillpress.com